I0796375

DEMOCRATICALLY APPLIED MACHINE

DEMOCRATICALLY APPLIED MACHINE

Robert Colman

Palimpsest Press
1171 Eastlawn Ave.
Windsor, Ontario. N8S 3J1
www.palimpsestpress.ca

Printed and bound in Canada
Cover design and book typography by Ellie Hastings
Edited by Jim Johnstone

Palimpsest Press would like to thank the Canada Council for the Arts and the Ontario Arts Council for their support of our publishing program. We also acknowledge the assistance of the Government of Ontario through the Ontario Book Publishing Tax Credit.

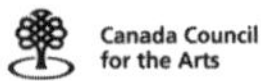

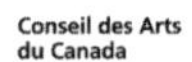

LIBRARY AND ARCHIVES CANADA CATALOGUING IN PUBLICATION

TITLE: Democratically applied machine / Robert Colman.
NAMES: Colman, Robert, 1973- author.
DESCRIPTION: Poems.
IDENTIFIERS: Canadiana (print) 20200172662
Canadiana (ebook) 20200172670

ISBN 9781989287439 (SOFTCOVER) | ISBN 9781989287446 (EPUB)
ISBN 9781989287453 (KINDLE) | ISBN 9781989287460 (PDF)

CLASSIFICATION: LCC PS8605.O473 D46 2020 | DDC C811/.6—DC23

TABLE OF CONTENTS

PART C: RUCK

PART D: HOLD

In Memoriam
Brian Colman (1933-2019)

MIDDLE DISTANCE

—after Gerhard Richter's
Landschaft bei Koblenz *(1987)*

Pure dark, you think,
could exist there,
haven of the animal
catalogue, expanse
of feral lung.

But this bucolic only feigns breadth.
Air dissembles the confluence ahead—
in cloud funk a tang of aluminum, gas
a boat
a barge.

Sure, earth as well, but the city breathes
hot on your wolf search,
claws glossed. On the hill
you are both not far enough
and too close. The problem,
Gerhard, is that your hill
is our heaven of non-committal,
echo-edged trees,

the hay field we can't quite see,
a memory-heat we can't glean—
thok of clogs on cobbles, vowels
stretched open on a spinning mule,
the pitch of rough cut steel on a lathe.

Sounds we hasten from.

Are saved from?

Muted, the soft-eye view
confuses the two. All
becomes other.

In his exiles
homeland,
memory,
father gives me pieces of willing
loss, our tools, phantom limbs.

We can forget so much
the pain has no name.

PART A: METAL

WHERE *DID* ALL THE JOB SHOPS GO?

The pup-like new town whelped
on a flat of good soil uncrowned—
acres we'd take, ton by ton,
to the south, north, east, west.
The map always pointing away.

The furrow fallows into breeze
block and red brick,
glass reflecting the light
of intersection after intersection.
A city-wide field of factories,

small warrens of good work.
Sure, I remember the union,
the shop steward, the time
card and camaraderie.
But we've fifteen-hundred square –

a handful of hombres, hopping
trade. No one knows us
outside necessity. Chance meeting
is for other places. Communities.
We're not really here—

always preparing what needs
to ship next, always highway
bound. Hand me those gloves,
that mask to bead the flat weld,
completion.

Mark your track
if you want to make it back—
you'll not recognize
where you've been. And the birds
you fail to hear? They left years ago.

GHOSTING THE ASSEMBLY LINE

Watch the car's body, trundled into place,
hands blurred, houring the births. History.
Quaint now, all those mouths that drawled
parts, paycheques, dinners, flatware sets.
As if our revolutions could still be fashioned,
wrench on wrench, turned in unison.

Take the minutes, now, transcribed notes
penned up the line, white lab coats. Sketch
the fingers that tool intention—Lean, Kanban,
black belts framed above large workstations,
intricate knots, each an action, the clean line
abstracting passion. The robots wave a greeting.

Hear the hum, second-hand vibrato accent
of the job shop floor. Work is done in smallness—
one part, four, more as required. As operator,
accountant, time hoarder. One man a workforce,
awaiting the order, more like us every day—
palms alighting on keyboards,

millling down the hours
into scrap.

THE MACHINE'S ADVICE

An erasure poem

Visualize the defect
in front of you.

Our display's going wrong.
This you can redo.

The setup, the root,
our hands?

We look up and down
around a nominal point.

Tool the line, go steadily
away from your tolerance.

Technology That Is Better,
help me feel. Data is useless.

You have a problem. And better
to know that—don't scrap
or blow up in the process.

That can happen.

The shop floor morning
is right there in the corner.

It's a large space,
another machine.

Stop and think
about how you are going.

To hopes, moment to moment.

Isn't the whole
that? The error happened
so you could learn more.

INTERVIEW WITH THE MACHINIST

He knows you have forgotten the first breath,
the blood and the cut cord.
Ask him. He could give you
that scream, the blade-freed shape.

He worries his clocks on commas, hyphens
of steel, bared bones and muscle
intuited in edge and thread.

Ask your questions. He shakes his head,
unable to conjure an airplane whole,
the haunches of an automobile,
a patriotic engine chugging a soft-shoe.

He's rehearsed *money, hours, margins*,
but thinks in the shape of the thing
that is nameless until it is freed,

his no-words turned clean in piecework births.

PART

Any of the manufactured objects
that are assembled together
to make a machine or instrument.

A quantity which,
together with others,
makes up a whole.

Involvement,
interest,
concern.

An act.

A share.

CAST IRON

Brittle, for all the orders given it
in sand, the free ferrite chafing
tight nodules, tough certainty.

Brute grey, all the black in the flame
given its heft, then coaxed
to tame completion—
one thread, maybe two,
transmission,
coupling,

Still only what you started with
at heart—a gentling out,
a sheen born against
imperfection.

Will it hold?
                    Always
the question.

UNEMPLOYED HOURLY

A cento

Do not lean on me, I'm still trying to find a job.
Victory is, we're exiting earth, we're leaving
all this dirt. Left to my own devices
I'd just sink into the soil.

I used to think there was a place—
hauling off the metal trays of stock,
the sun going down in the mouths of the furnaces,
lead slugs and blue smoke in the moon—
I would stand at the centre of a room
with winch and ropes and hooks, to wrangle
intensity, to gather, bloom
as one long word,
one hard prayer
this work
just beginning.

I keep trying to remember that this
is my life now—the language of
the unsaid. My favourite pages.

FEALTY (A PIPE WELDER AND HIS RIG)

People think, it's just a welder,
hundred foot of cable,
ten feet of whip on the end,
exact same stinger. You'd suppose.
But no, I got my own rig,
need to know she'll stay lit
when I'm whipping the rod,
can't have her snub on ya,
can't have the electrode glass over,
freeze—leads to stubbing,
porosity. I got 45 on the truck,
55 on the arm, and they furnish,
but three repairs and I'm kickin'
stones, simple. I gotta know
she's mine, no one else's.
I seen her kind built—man named George
been winding armatures near
forty years. Can't say it's quite a snowflake
but partly handmade, fires how I like,
how his tools set her so
when I'm one half of a tie-in,
12 o'clock to six on an alligator bite,
I'm skatin' her in there, only watching
the lightning, a storm of stupid, all
shades of fucked up on the other side
as the other guy's arcs fly. Yup,
hundred foot o' cable,
ten feet o' whip,
her stinger,
my arm.

FROM THE FRONT

On Black Friday the fiber laser started cutting Christmas cards, etching the addresses of world leaders on their edges. The fierce hiss of the doped optical amplified on metal met us that morning, the lasers having made their own hour for this. The American President received the silhouette of a reindeer, the Canadian PM the shadow of mistletoe. And for every member of the National People's Congress, the track marks of a sleigh on an empty hill. We watched the first sheet slide from the machine, dutifully broke the tabbed edges and set each piece of aluminum on the bench top, calculating postage, estimating travel times. Our foreman found a bell to ring, started whistling *Winter Wonderland*. The machine was going half-speed, but we'd clock right to our own business at nine, which seemed half-thought-through in comparison, although who has the money for postage? No, I love a machine with ideas, but I was thinking enclosures and wall brackets, a well-honed geometry. I liked the card for the German Chancellor best—just a hand and a snowball, mid-arc, *Joyeux Noël* melting into a Babel of air.

THE ANGELS DESCEND TO FILL THE SKILLS GAP

And so it was told
that we would commandeer the ghost stations
and free the controls. From the womb
we would speak G code and the constant strain
of knowing without being told, having known
hours that had yet to be invented.
We would read the clocks to you as we entered,
work luck from the weeks you worried for,
the billables you had no faith to believe.
We are coming back for you because
we couldn't come forward through black light,
the fear you worried like God
your own fragile existence
so much bigger than us.

WHITE COLLAR

The problem was ever assuming a difference.
Owning your own labour is never sufficient.

PART B: PULL

CUTTING FOR THE LAYMAN

1. Mill

Absence isn't synonymous with lack. The lock's
body. Mouths of empty cups. The time before
diagnosis. Considered hollows:

2. Turn

every tussle a circle. Fat snow of words funneled
to choice line. Shouts cowed by doubt. Return
to where we began. Flushed, renewed, less of
us better, not lack. Driver pins poised to move
through the lock's body

3. Drill

as our bodies key love. Compulsion in double
time, wanting *in* and *through*. Desire a word in the
next room. How we see ourselves

4. Tap

in threads—an anchored conclusion. That next
room her story on a childhood hillside. The cup
I retrieve from it, slipped gently into a pocket.
Another tumbler placed.

PARTS

A personal quality or attribute; an ability.
A party, a body of adherents; a faction.
Side in a contract, contest, question.
In part, partly, to some extent.
A portion of a country.
Parting, leave-taking.
A physical side;
the genitals.

LET US BUTT HEADS, LOVE

A cento

I fell into the flowers feeling for fractures
when you said *pony* and I whispered *mountain*.

We had sour red wine and empty stomachs
and came back with a mind full of bric-a-brac,

not caring anymore what might snap in its jaw,
the sun going down in the mouths of the furnaces.

Teach me to dance. We have no music here.
Evening crickets scatter through the chronic care facility.

And only now as the tears start do you smile.
Why fight fair, then? Let connections run wild.

Backdrop after backdrop of stars
and you hold up a bumper crop of cars.

The barren, astonished earth
fraught in the works, turning the gear of custom.

TRADE SHOW SECRETS

It's all in the cloud, they say,
know-how no longer necessary.

Well, someone still has to know something,
but they're not here, not you or me.

I can tell you where the German U-boat washed ashore,
how aged balsamic plays nicely on a Piedmontese nut.

Not good enough? I can splice a pre-roll with thirteen
seconds mill time into an ideal pitch for efficiency.

No need for the go-go girls in plastic boots,
but the guys like them when they pretend to play violin.

Isn't this a reward? Hell yes, in spandex!
We're tired. Surely we've made enough of this world.

CHOOSING HER TRADE

The corridor is hers, she's told, every
claim paid or waylaid, the adjuster's
wink crimping the sunk IN tray,
lengths of Gyproc she tries to guess,
counting as she guides a fingernail
along either wall wing
and walks to offices she's told
might be hers in the offing.

So many eyes she imagines
aching from this glass tomb
out to the skyline, to rasped sound
unbound by white noise, snow-dirt
drum of thumbs on PCs, leaked
hint of sweat in the sterility.

Own wound two ways in elastics
at her wrist, she counts
twelve slabs of sheetrock
that end in this, one nail,
her index, marking an imperfection
she aches to fix.
Aches to own
just this.

AFTER LOWRY, AFTER CORNISH

This shop is no longer akin
to working the coalface.

The flat cap is stacked
on the hat stand, decorous.

The whistle blows inside,
though we don't recall
where, or how it began.

Nothing is seen as a need,
as such, so need wallows,
a word at sea, and we are
all walking away from seeing.

We are all walking away
without fibres to stitch up our lungs,
dust and lime a tickle of history.
The factories are condos now.
We know them to close the doors.

In the painting… if this were a painting…
we are all walking away, hatless,
in snow that is only our snow.
In fact, there are many canvases—single
man or woman in each, backs turned,
covered in their own muslin cloths.

So quiet, you'd like to think it were
the end of something, a noble exit,
which was what we always wanted,
wasn't it? Serenity, of a sort.
Nothing makes a sound in these paintings
White silence. The counsel of one.
But then, what is home?

WHALE HUNT

"If this breaks you die." —A job shop owner cradling an airplane part in his hands.

We ask you to pull us
further from land,
harpoon snug in your side,
seal bladder
ballast above you.

We ask after we leap
from our boats
and pierce your flesh –
carry our skiffs
as far as your might allows.

Let me roll my bones,
clack the dominoes back in place.
There is not one leviathan
we do not love
unto death. Who drew

whom into the deeps?
Wasn't everything
necessity? I carved a compass
on a scrimshaw box
because direction

was all I could think,
wind and current
and your back as it breached.
If I must now
put away my blade

I would still follow you,
all the tow ropes
stretching unseen
from bulwark and mast, cliff side
and the gaff sail of earth

pounded solid, this doorway.

THE MACHINE AT REST

The engine's disengaged
but the body echoes, miles
of highway become
a skin-hum. The ear inured,
yet also harmed, I'm sure.

We forget into the world, move from task to task
scheme to scheme. Decibels and tools redeemed
by others, yet not left in the making, late at night,

hands still shaking.

PART C: RUCK

SON TO FATHER

Problem is, I played by the book
and now I'm just marionetting my story:
nature, nurture, half lies just as like,
but I follow string to elbow or knee—
one day I landed in a schoolyard,
walked from there to here, kicking curbs and doors.
This isn't pin-the-blame-on-the-senior.

Problem is, I keep living backwards.
Maybe if I string up this puppet
it can karaoke the memories
as I get on with clearing other scrap
it unveils. There's a line to happy,
I'm sure. Problem is, it includes books you read me
and the rest we both groped for blindly.

BONE

Bone's shadow is more solid than itself.
I mine the nerve-scape of the past
for some fractal of health
to explain bone / shadow. Warn? React.

Telephone teases shadow most weeks.
Before calling, I'd gauge fragility.
Would he be garrulous with chips and whiskey
or grunt out? What of me would cleave?

When everything he said was dismissive
I saw the disappearance of us
as foreign enemy or phantom limb,
cack-handed apparatus.

At close quarters, he simplifies with a word:
clarity with a boot through pressboard.

HALF MOON

Words score a hole in the pressboard door
my sister slams shut. The shouting's put away.

The half moon stays
on the door long enough I don't remember
what the red of morning is supposed to be.
Habit is partly assumption—this *is* what *is*,
poor, unfinished.

Don't tell, don't tell.

Even now,
I eye the hallway to my parents' bedroom,
brush shadows away. Who's in charge?
I creep, count distance in steps, volume,
decide it's not my door, but maybe my moon.

Mum, mum,

stay mum.

REC ROOM

"Good evening ladies and gentlemen"
he almost whispers. A confidence? Dave Allen
leans into the rec room, drink enjoined,
cheerleader for the fallen man.
Dave talks about women
but he is pre-woman, all priest,
the gag of incompetence
where he, my father and I meet,
laughter of red face and teeth,
smoke whir of the air purifier.
I get out of bed for this, sneak
downstairs into the TV's flicker
where the only shout is Allen's,
our words too keyed to explosions.

PERIMETER

Streetlights stand where no street is laid,
a patchwork pattern on truck-milled ground
that confuses the lines the farmhouse made
or sanctuary the adjacent church allowed.

It's dawn when I drive out to pace
this borderland's suburban dry rot.
The contours of a cornfield chase
gaps that await drywall, wives, dogs.

I believe I yearn for countryside,
framing clapboard and tin roof for a grainy snap,
but enjoy the collapse—black and white
images imagined as living map

in fact an assurance of safe return,
anomalies frozen, picked like sunburn.

DEPRESSION

"Beautiful day, eh babe? Eh babe?" I prattle,
pacing a small square of beach
and watching her kneel on the flats, eyes muzzled
to her work, sculpting mythical beasts,
gods with mouths set to blow winds out to sea
to settle… something? I can't know, though want
too much to know and she just wants to be.
She reaches methodically for sand
while I review protocols for happy—
comedy, seduction, sex, appeasement—
feet in crab puddles. I watch, shut the fuck up,
but ache to save her from her absence.

Fool.

The sun god's face multiplies, knotted brows
grow finer as she grips his chin in her toes.

GOOD, BETTER

A good absence? I can't see it clear
when I've seen her self-portraits—face a blank
gash above a body that glowers
about her sex, as if she bled this ink.

Silence? I know it as prelude, postlude,
a worry place for the tension to build
into a scruff-faced bully attitude,
and think *safety, talking, kissing, bed*.

Yap like the smallest dog in the street, boy!
Nip her heels, dance around her legs!
*Let's play tennis, let's fuck, let me read you
to sleep*. Pant a forced laugh, almost beg

to be her hero, thinking yourself good,
force-feeding her this fantasy sainthood.

FATHER TO SON

Was I meant to play the saint? I don't know.
The God of I Don't Know, that's what I knew.
I remember cheering you to the goal
at hockey, all the days I didn't have to choose

to do or be anything. I was just there,
and the days happened. But hours alone,
in my head, mid-Atlantic, I feared
my self and my loss. What is home?

I know you think that's a simple question,
but it doesn't take an ocean to confuse it,
merely time, the ego's expectations
meeting the fear of its limits.

In the midst of it you set an example,
mistakes threaded into involuntary muscle.

Love,

WAKING

A cento

From some sky an inch above the mattress, I would
answer every question with a biblical quotation—
one woman, then another, then another.
Deep from within the changing colours of a life
like no cold I'd previously experienced,
trying to tell me the one true story of my life
– an impostor, even to myself. Except
the windows, worn to a shiver, let in rain
and the reflection in the water, it burned!

THE PARTY

—a sestina after Michelangelo Antonioni's film La Notte

The excuse for abandon is a torrent of water.
A train passes, he stands in the road
and on the car roof rain lays a braid
twining endlessly the hood, the door.
The rain is presence separate from sky,
every man / woman who "just can't" in its hold.

It repeats in him, that jingle, "to have and to hold,"
until it is nonsensical bumpf, a drumming of water
drops become a child's chant to the summer sky.
Through traffic lights in the city's heart he rode
the words to silence, tried to ignore his want to adore
vaguely, someone—soft nap of braid

on a new young woman, a braid
he sniffs like a vampire and aches to hold
like the sexually possessed teen he isn't now, dor-
mouse claws on the body of a skulking water
rat. Scrub has buried the familiar railroad
ties. This is no longer his sky.

He can't picture it now, the sky-
scraper arrogance his romance owned. He abraded
the sentimental years ago, watched anger erode
his fellow feelings. He thought its last hold
had disappeared, passed like water
at a drunken party. But maybe there is a trap door

that opens as his host / lover leaves him on the door-
step and walks away into the house's maze. Whisky
breath fogs his head, but his shadow floats in the water-
clear stillness of a fountain. One ripple would upbraid
his body, and all the errors he can't stop holding
would be erased and allow him to selflessly erode.

Ha! Wouldn't he love that? Probably no. He outrode
romance. He goes to find his wife. Love is fealty, is a dor-
mant memory of the act, sometimes, have / hold
knotted among the branches, shot through the musky
rot of dawn as he walks next to her, taut braid
of them, while their oaths and curses, flame to water.

The film corrodes. He knows the sky
sounds of leaves but is also door, time, river's braid. Ego.
Theirs hold shakily at the waterline.

SEASONAL AFFECTIVE DISORDER

(or, dreaming the clawfoot's crash—an escape fantasy)

It was the initial slip that surprised,
my pimpled backside colliding
slantways with the tub bottom
as it untucked itself, to slide
through the rot and tin-thin walls,
slalom ground-ways
across the sunroom roof.

Armageddon of the mind is so slow—
ice-rimed, I thought, blue-palmed
and patient as stone, I thought.

And I thought.
But no, it was worse than thought,
sitting still in the frost-
wash, the glassy light tightening
the sheen on this hairless skinflint.
No longer thinking, I chucked
a bit of rot windward
from this old cottage.

No spanner to rudder and drum
the basin's sides—so free
it made for fence and tree root,
and my chest, shuddering
wing flap and tantrum,
nippled to the audacity
of the chain link's reveal.

Sodden thunk as it stabbed the trunk,
blackened wet in the slow dreck of thaw.
A toe to the snow-mash, leaning
against the tap-mast, the worry knot,
the wallow now pierced in chiding air.
Salt-grimed and squinting in the sun,
looking for a new door through which to run.

WHERE WE TAKE IT

Nearly hit a porcupine last night
but I was thirtyish safe on the straight lanes
and the wind fierced me quiet in the swerve.

I'd found our road, which surprised you.
Dark was dark, and the trees were sleeping.

Earlier, you had imagined mafia making rough
in a Camaro
and I was liking the open road less and less.
I took on the threat, gave it an engine, wondered
where next.

The town shunted its hull lakeside,
a harbourmaster's bottled shout.

The rain was warm. No need to change
our clothes or run for cover.
We dropped our knives,
blades nuzzling the weave.

WHEN IT WAS TIME TO LEAVE

For months I wrote only one scene, over and over:
a man bent into a storm, wind-lash exposing ribs—
his umbrella a punched lung.

Always a man with a Mao collar,
the umbrella's colour changing
from red to black and back again.

I thought I was looking at him
from my bed, the glass of the bookcase
collecting the storm,
the duvet tucked beneath my chin.

But, truthfully, I was caught
in the seam of his collar,
thick monsoon air smudging me
into the fabric,
my ear awaiting orders.

PLEASE WRITE SOON

The city has broken into my childhood
home, defaced the family
photos, scored
our fixed smiles.

Who said we could be anything?

That sickness, memory
locked the hotel door,
leaving me this slight
window, empty inbox.

PART D: HOLD

THE PAINTING

(Salford)

You never see the machines,
only smoke, red brick chimney,
Stockport viaduct, a stadium.
Not strict landscape—no landscape
precisely this in Lancashire
but Lowry and Dad agree to it.
The shape fits a winnowing,
pedestrians gather for a portrait
then forget. Whose hat is this?
Whose pipe? Is he a soldier?
Dad squints at the white/grey sky.
A horsecart trundles away, familiar.
Has the crowd thinned? Doddered off?
He falls asleep into a knowing
which is more poetry than fact
now that facts are ricochet.
The elisions fuse shut, a scumble sets
new streetscapes, make him safe.

"Dad, describe it to me."

SLIPPING TIME

(High Peak / Saltersford / Stonehenge)

Father's bike is at the edge of a field.

Whitewashed pub on a Cheshire hill,
grandpa's Woodbines a static will
boxed in a cabinet of the near-forgotten
and dad against the bar's blackened
beam, slouched frieze of family
history, Lilliputian cigarettes, nub end
of a man I never met. Vague whiff of lager.
Memory a monument suspect as any wager.

The pedal's stuck fast in the grass.

Dad loves this pub, cupped nook in the map
of lore he might half know if told - Saltersford,
its valley cut close between the bar
and silk-made Macc. A dale cast in stars,
demons, shifting stones—to him, unknown
but in blood tones, the earthen track,
like the canal's towpath
feeding all the undergods of home.

The grass is still wet. Morning near the circle.

Own. He names Norbury Hollow, Three
Purse Lane, the rail track,
the miners' placid cottages, gentles me
"drive slow if you're not ready
for the road," which he knows—
House of Twelve Windows, blood map
of ring roads, coping the edges
of today, unbidden tomorrow.

At 16, he walks through the stones, unimpeded.

Buckle the map—grandpa a phone operator
in Stone, Ministry orders after closures,
seniority. And where the cancer would eat. Buckle
now and then, the stones moving to quench
a thirst, it is said, to fill ancient need,
if we could hear them from this snug,
where we try a local pint or two, repeat,
where we don't know how to ask for clarity.

And this spinning, the weight of the chain.

Dad now threatens to forget daily, to sink
from knowing, himself a valley. Here
those stones to drink, his parents and sister.
Rothman's, DuMaurier, and after
pneumonia, sleep, rye and ginger,
red wine. In case this needs not be forgotten,
the stones the lists we make of the unbidden,
the undertimes he gives us in the blood-patter.

The motion of him dropping it in the grass repeats.

Saltersford's chapel has a hearth—odd,
as if it weren't to be a church,
or the newly faithful thought this was god
and what he would want—embers
to chase the holy. Not really so contrary.
We collect and scatter, and collect again.
We circle, hunting for the blood-name, true tell,
looking for a place to prop our bikes.

"We just left our bikes by the side of the road," he says,
"Walked straight through the stones.
No one there."

WALKING LONGSHAW

(Peak District)

We didn't make the grindstone lane
at property's southern edge –
chiseled hands discarded, haphazard
at quarry's end. We had lodge tea,
Victoria sponge, swept the artificial
lake, some sheep, sepia teen soldiers
convalescing by a guidestoop furring
a sunken path. Everything clean finished
or fading, gathered by north gate.

I don't know what father will remember
today—he takes notes each evening
for recall, training his catch hand. And really,
how long will I take to lose sparse
minutes in Boggart's Hollow,
bull-braced wind in the thatch of trees?
I was pleased we walked as far as we did,
dad swerved but steady enough on his pins,
strode out, unheeded, unheld.

Yet I return also to what wasn't.
Millstones passed over for the French
quartz bur, the German cullen,
coining moss eyes in grandfather
earth. Grave markers,
stale currency. How I want
this fake memory as much
as the real, to round out
the joint discovery
of our leaving.

FICKLE GODS

(Haddon Hall, Derbyshire)

More shade than stone, the chapel's fresco secco
vines have faded to pencil sketches. From how
you grip your hat, I see you're smitten.
Your atheist heart permits some allowance

for patiently-worked faith. You know hardness,
carve dream hypotheses—long study in your lab,
petri dishes, a single cell's forty year animus
to corral your days, half-defining the life lived,

those hours, deft cigarette at the fume hood,
yellowed press clippings on an office door,
impermanence a knowledge that leaves you
more ether than words. You blink now, stare

as the allure of air baffles you out to the garden wall.
Amnesiac, here: a view of static, 400-year-old crucible.

OLD FRIENDS

(Stockport)

I think we're away to the pub
when Dad legs a quick pivot aft of me,
determined, beyond the brewery's stables,
beetling across the tombstone walk,
out to the empty fall behind St. Mary's church,
iron fence posts framing his stare.

I chase the lane, unsure for us both.

"Cornbrook Chemical was here," he states,
the names of the dead fading underfoot.
"They made paint colours,
spring-fed works, like Robinson's across
the road." His old workplace,
1950 or so, snatched back into the air.

Film on film. Is knowing more precious
when tenuous? A musk of then-now
well housed in the ground survey,
we pace downhill to the Arden Arms,
the snug, the stopped grandfather clock,
him less agitated now he's seen, or been...

What to call staring at blank space
and carving from it your need?
Good ghosts, when you know where to look,
can walk steady past God
and feel solid red brick.

MARKET DAY

(Leek)

Saturday is adult nursery bric-a-brac, yesterday's tack—Victorian smut, Bakelite dud lamps, train sets and epaulets, lighting distant memories. And we're *Boy's Own* explorers, poachers, egg-handed anthropologists of commerce. Red brick claps hard the hills, and out comes lack—that standing still we feel when we want to be thrown forward or back in time, the line between making and made. But there's a time-bothered plastic gate keeping us penned in our today. We buy a book at the library, 10 p. "Let's get s_me b_con butties," dad says. In a blond wood pub, desultory modernity pared from the square—we try to ignore the sheen, the plate glass reality, look to the cobbles outdoors, return a milky dream. Here, the street we pilfered for *Factory*, still disappearing next a string of antique shops. "N_ce horse br_sses, St_ffordshire maps. 'm sure I've got one as like at h_me." My 81-year-old father dodges traffic, unsteady, "t_me fer t_a." I try to see streets clear of the car park, clear of years, with track suits and scruff a dozen paces away watching me fluff this scene into absent-serene. Dad, can we keep you? What can we want together, perhaps I ask—these brasses on a strip of leather, a picture of that Morris Marina in a flashback flipbook? "________" Maybe Alan Garner's patch of local fantasy will hold you engaged. "He's an odd b_rd, ‘n’t he?” Pleasantly waylaid in this body. Cousin Alex buys a plastic torch, shabby-chic accessory. “All this j_nk, agh!” you growl. All of us looking for a past satisfactory and passive. I shadow you on the stairs of the stationer’s, this week’s protocol, understood or not, to be there, whether there is some folded space-time in a knot of shops, or the certainty of a glass. These days are for wavering, hailing what passes, calling down, holding fast.

SLEEPING

(High Lane)

Thick time, fog of days
thins on his papery lips,

seesaw cloth at the chest
as breath gets trapped,
wrestling the lung cage,
the exhale that won't come

until, out of silence, he gasps,
panting, stumbling
a path through the hedge-
row of body,

like his mind now,
traitorous.

TRUST

(Salisbury)

"Can we leave this house now?"
he asks from the window, looking
for familiar landmarks—a car,
a route to safety? Panic.

"It's a hotel, Dad.
Salisbury, UK,
it's OK, we'll leave
in the morning."

He's unconvinced. And thin. I forget
that this is how he's always been,
the red of his neck, the blue-white sunken
chest, boy-like and smooth.

But he's all suspicion now,
staring at the crumpled bed.
"Who's been sleeping here?"
Again, panic.

"You dad, it's your bed.
It's alright, time for sleep."
And very slowly he climbs
into a thin cocoon of trust.

Twice in the night I coax him
away from the open window,
try firm but casual, as if
we've always had such exchanges,

think of the cathedral lawn
that, earlier, he'd sighed in awe—
the spire aloft in Constable blue,
wish for a god so perfectly hewn.

PROTEST

(Manchester)

Fuck this loss. Moth-bled dusk,
toss away this able coat.

Pins don't mark this word suit,
this scar-shot mind. Papa,

want this nail-hole
self, base aura.

Moan from this bone-sure cage
what urge paws—pine rush,

wolf ache,
fist hard rain.

Call loud
undo, undo.

WATCHING

A cento

(Ludlow)

When he had fallen deep asleep and was snoring,
when the baby face and old serious one
tarnished in the moistness,
gone small, thin salt and blind with tears.

What a life he would have lived without them
in this democratically applied machine.
He hid behind books, and
thunder lay down in the heart.

Everything is lost in the fire
and lost in the gauging. Fire
he will grope back into
and crouch down.

FATHER, MISSING IN THE CATHEDRAL

(Worcester)

He slips from view, not present,
de-limbed hitchhiker gone offside.
Loss occurs perverse. He elides
into quips of memory—endless holes.

I crypt-check the prince's tomb,
the choir, the cloisters, 'round King
John's prone, stiff body. Rock, dust, stone—
how little I become with every step.

Elders? We need new epithets
for the howl you build in your ineptness—
you've visited this church, right?
Little child keening for doll

or superhero while every elder opens
your chest, climbs in, settles, pulls
close to the chosen rib, clings, sings,
umpteen sets of teeth you won't weep for:

don't trust. Totter off beyond the tight
knots of your shoes. Poor, silly boy,
your ounce of love twisted to fright,
the world is just this church.

Just this church, you tell yourself
once more. But inside you feel them
perch. It's possible you'll joke
over dinner, mock your upset,

but for now everywhere yells
yet,
yet,
yet.

NOTES

"The Machine's Advice" was created using an article in the magazine *Metalworking Production & Purchasing*.

"Part" and "Parts" are both found poems that take their definitions from *The Shorter Oxford English Dictionary*.

"Unemployed Hourly" takes lines from the following poems:

Black Nikes, Harryette Mullen
God is President, She's the Rose of the World, Ana Božičević
Personals, C.D. Wright
Eden, then and now, Ruth Stone
Coming Close, Philip Levine
The Foundry Garden, Stanley Plumly
The Royal Botanical Gardens, Adam Getty
The Telephonist, Susan Yuzna
Hay for the Horses, Gary Snyder
Sending Flowers, Hannah Stephenson
Calling him back from layoff, Bob Hicok
This Work, Martha Zweig
Scenes of Life at the Capital, Philip Whalen
The Glass Essay (Liberty), Anne Carson

"Fealty (A Pipe Welder And His Rig)": a "stinger" is a welding gun; "45 on the truck, 55 on the arm" means he's being paid a certain amount for his equipment (on the truck) and his skill. Gas, rods and bottles would be "furnished"; "tie-in"—a difficult weld in pipeline work where you're bringing two ends of a pipeline together. It means you have to cut one pipe to fit the other, which is awkward and means the ends aren't going to fit snug—there'll be varied gaps that need to be filled during the weld. If the pipe is large enough, two welders will work on it at once, opposite sides of the pipe.

"Let Us Butt Heads, Love" takes lines from the following poems:

It's Spring Again, David McFadden
You Never Seemed So Human, Matthea Harvey
Burned, Philip Levine
Disintegration, James Arthur
My God, It's Full of Stars, Tracy K. Smith
The Foundry Garden, Stanley Plumly
Alabanza: In Praise of Local 100, Martin Espada
Orderlies, Gabe Foreman
Forgiveness, Alan Shapiro
A Moral Climate, Walid Bitar
Roman Candle, David McFadden
Insect Dust, Noel Black

Laurence Stephen "L.S." Lowry (1 November 1887–23 February 1976) was an English artist born in Stretford, Lancashire. Lowry is famous for painting scenes of life in the industrial districts of North West England in the mid-20th century.

Norman Stansfield Cornish (18 November 1919–1 August 2014) was the last surviving member of the "Pitman's Academy" art school at the Spennymoor Settlement in County Durham,

North East England. A former coal miner, he was known for his pictures of mining community life.

"Waking" takes lines from the following poems:

Her First Week, Sharon Olds
The New Presbytery, Westport, County Mayo, Paul Durcan
Another Muse, Frederick Seidel
Undo It, Carl Phillips
The Same Cold, Stephen Dunn
Prayer, Marie Howe
The Possible, Raymond Carver
Moving House, Robin Robertson
I tell my doctor…, Tua Forsstrom (Translated by David McDuff)

"Watching" quotes lines from the following poems:

From My Father's Side Of The Bed, Marie Howe
Fathers, Al Purdy
Lead, Russell Thornton
Fathers, Patrick Lane
A Good Father, Michael Ryan
A Man Takes His Daughter, Age Five, To A Public Execution By Guillotine, Paris, 1857, Thomas Lux
Evasive Maneuvers, Billy Collins
A Boy, John Ashbery
Burning and Fathering: Accounts of My Country, Jack Gilbert
The Daughters Singing to Their Father, Paul Durcan

ACKNOWLEDGEMENTS

A selection of these poems was collected in a limited edition chapbook, *Factory* (Frog Hollow Press 2015). Versions appear in the sections "Metal" and "Pull".

"Middle Distance" was the recipient of a 2018 *Vallum* Award For Poetry and was published in *Vallum* issue 16:1.

"Ghosting the Assembly Line" and "When it was time to leave" appeared in *EVENT*.

Earlier versions of "Part", "Parts" and "Where Did All The Job Shops Go?" appeared on the CanadianPoetries.com website.

Versions of "Unemployed Hourly" and "Fealty (A Pipe Welder And His Rig)" appeared in *Hamilton Arts & Letters*.

"Where We Take It" appeared in issue 119 of *Poetry Ireland Review*.

"Whale Hunt" was chosen for the League of Canadian Poets' *Poem in Your Pocket* selection in 2017.

"Old Friends" was a finalist for *The Malahat Review*'s 2017 Open Season Awards. It appeared in *Grain Magazine*.

"Fickle Gods" appeared in *Contemporary Verse 2*.

"Trust" and "Sleeping" appeared in *The Dalhousie Review*.

"Bone" and "Perimeter" appeared in *The Salzburg Review*.

"Half Moon" appeared in *The Fiddlehead*.

"The Painting" appeared in *Vallum*.

Thanks to Jim Johnstone for believing in this collection and welcoming me into the Palimpsest fold. Thanks also to the whole Palimpsest team for the work you do for Canadian poetry.

I owe a great debt of gratitude to Shane Neilson, who not only published a section of this book as editor at Frog Hollow Press but helped me shape the rest of it at a time when it had lost its way.

To the Muse Co-operative, thanks for taking the time with early versions of many of these poems.

Thanks to my family for always being supportive of my work.

Last but not least, love to Kristi and the clowder for making home a place where this is all made possible.

ABOUT THE AUTHOR

Robert Colman is a Newmarket, Ont.-based writer and editor. He has been involved in trade publications for the manufacturing industry for more than ten years. Colman is the author of two other full-length collections of poetry, *Little Empires* (Quattro Books 2012) and *The Delicate Line* (Exile Editions 2008), and the chapbook *Factory* (Frog Hollow Press 2015). He received his MFA from UBC in 2016.